DRAWING AWESOME
INSECTS

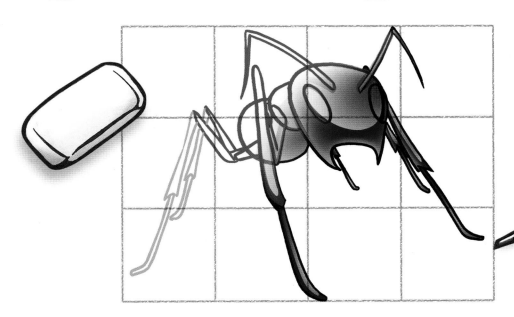

Damien Toll

WINDMILL
BOOKS

Contents

Introduction

Drawing is a fun and rewarding hobby for both children and adults alike. This book is designed to show how easy it is to draw great pictures by building them in simple stages.

What you will need

Only basic materials are required for effective drawing. These are:

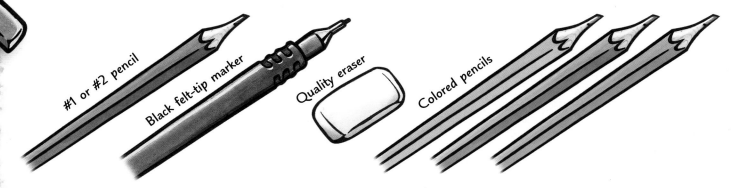

#1 or #2 pencil

Black felt-tip marker

Quality eraser

Colored pencils

These will be enough to get started. Avoid buying the cheapest pencils. Their leads often break off in the sharpener, even before they can be used. The leads are also generally too hard, making them difficult to see on the page.

Cheap erasers also cause problems by smudging rather than erasing. This often leaves a permanent stain on the paper. By spending a little more on art supplies in these areas, problems such as these can be avoided.

When purchasing a black marker, choose one to suit the size of your drawings. If you draw on a large scale, a thick felt-tip marker may be necessary. If you draw on a medium scale, a medium-point marker will do and if on a small scale, a 0.3 mm, 0.5 mm, 0.7 mm, or 0.8 mm felt-tip marker will work best.

The Stages

Simply follow the lines drawn in orange on each stage using your #1 or #2 pencil. The blue lines on each stage show what has already been drawn in the previous stages.

1.

2.

3.

In the final stage the drawing has been outlined in black and the simple shape and wire-frame lines erased. The shapes are only there to help us build the picture. We finish the picture by drawing over the parts we need to make it look like our subject with the black marker, and then erasing all the simple shape lines.

Included here is a sketch of a bee as it would be originally drawn by an artist.

These are how all the insects in this book were originally worked out and drawn. The orange and blue stages you see above are just a simplified version of this process. The drawing here has been made by many quick pencil strokes working over each other to make the line curve smoothly. It does not matter how messy it is as long as the artist knows the general direction of the line to follow with the black marker at the end. The pencil lines are erased and a clean outline is left. Therefore, do not be afraid to make a little mess with your #1 or #2 pencil, as long as you do not press so hard that you cannot erase it afterwards.

4.

5.

Grids made of squares are set behind each stage in this book. Make sure to draw a grid lightly on your page so it does not press into the paper and show up after being erased. Artist tips have also been added to show you some simple things that can make your drawing look great. Have fun!

Ant

Ants can be found just about anywhere in the world, working together to collect food for their colony. The queen ant spends almost her whole life laying eggs. They use their antennae to smell. Ants don't have lungs! They breathe through tiny holes that they have all over their body.

1.

Begin by drawing a grid with four equal squares going across and three down.

Then draw the slightly coned shape for the head. Draw a smaller semicircle for the middle part of the body. Add another circle behind that for the rear part of the body.

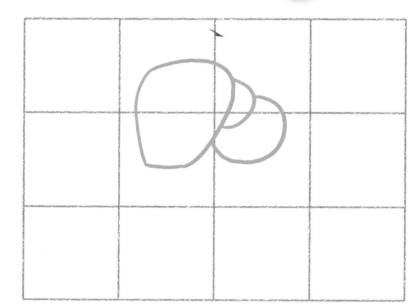

2.

Add the two eyes on the first shape and the arch at the bottom of this shape. Draw in the shapes for the legs. Check that your drawing is in the correct place on the grid before you move on.

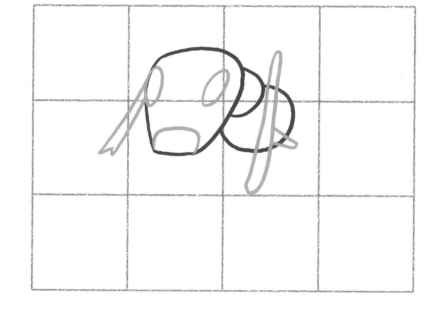

3.

Here we add the antennae and some more parts for the legs.

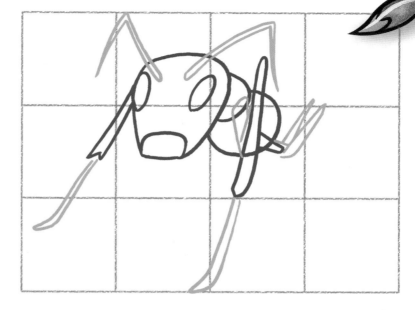

4.

Finish this drawing with the rest of the leg parts. Remember when outlining your ant to only go over the lines needed and erase all the construction lines.

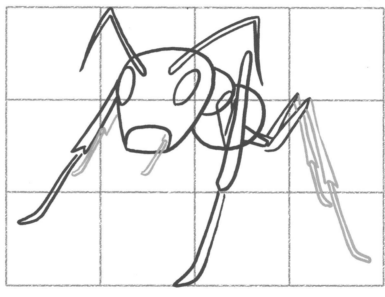

5.

Here we have a "flea's-eye view" looking up at the ant. We thought it would be fun to take a different angle on the ant because they are very small and usually looked upon from a great height. By taking a different view, we can make something look more interesting.

Wasp

Usually baby wasps will grow up inside a wasp nest, but some wasps lay their eggs inside other insects. That host insect will slowly be eaten by the baby wasp as it grows up. Wasps generally eat other insects, but some species are vegetarian. Watch out for this fiendish character, it has a very nasty sting!

1.

Begin by drawing a grid with three equal squares going across and down.

Now draw the two smaller eye shapes. Add the head circle behind these. Finally add the tall oval behind the head shape for the body.

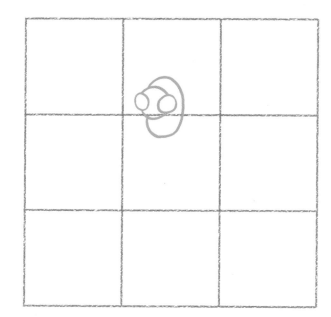

2.

Draw the wings coming out of the oval body. Add a thin waist piece and a large bulb for the abdomen and stinger. Check that your shapes are correct before moving on.

3.

Here we draw some lines (or wire frames) for the six legs. The legs will be built around these. Draw a circle at the end of the middle set of legs for the hands. Add some lines for the wings. Finish with the details on the wasp's face.

4.

Draw the top of the neck above the head shape. Add some razor sharp teeth. On the circle for the hand, add a zig-zagged line for the fingers. Build the legs in separate pieces around the wire-frame lines that were drawn in the previous stage.

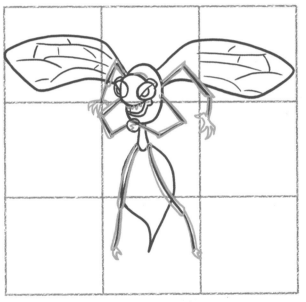

5.

Wasps are very bright and easy to see with their distinctive black and yellow markings. Did you know black and yellow are the two strongest contrasting colors?

Praying Mantis

The praying mantis is a master of disguise. It camouflages itself to look like a leaf while it sneaks up on its prey. It's called a "praying" mantis because its front legs are folded in a position that makes it look like it is praying. The mantis eats other insects and sometimes even small birds!

1.

Begin by drawing a grid with four equal squares going across and two down.

Then draw a triangular shape in the top left corner of the grid. Now draw the circular shape at the other end. Join these two shapes with a line. The thin body will be based on this line.

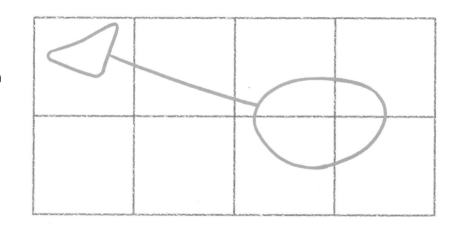

2.

Draw shapes for eyes on either side of the triangle. Draw around the long line and smoothly join it on to the body shape, coming to a point at the rear.

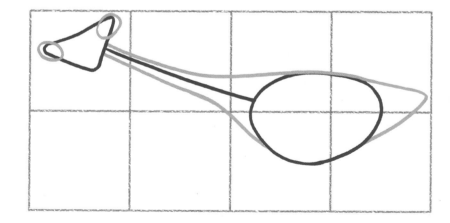

3.

Add the front leg. Draw in the middle leg and the wing.

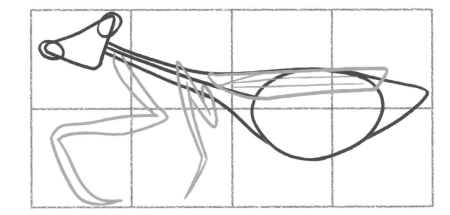

4.

Draw in the back leg and the body lines. Notice on the bottom they have been made to look slightly lumpy. Draw in the legs on the other side to finish.

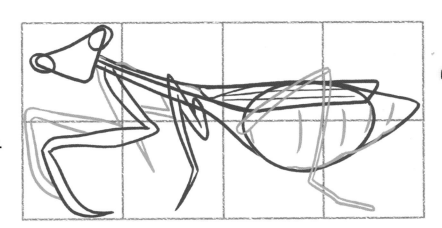

5.

The praying mantis is mostly green with a little gray on the side of its belly. You could draw it on a leaf or on a tree branch, as we have.

Ladybug

Ladybugs range from 1 to 10 mm, less than ½ inch, in length. Although they are called ladybugs, there are both males and females in the species. It is very hard to tell the difference between a male and a female ladybug. They have brightly colored backs. When they are being attacked, they ooze a yellow fluid out of their joints to make them smell and taste bad to a predator. Some ladybugs live for about two years.

1.

Begin by drawing a grid with three equal squares going across and down.

Now draw a roundish shape. Be careful to notice where the shape intersects points on the grid.

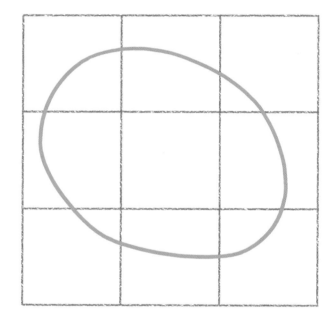

2.

Draw in some lines to divide the shape into the head and two parts of the ladybug's back.

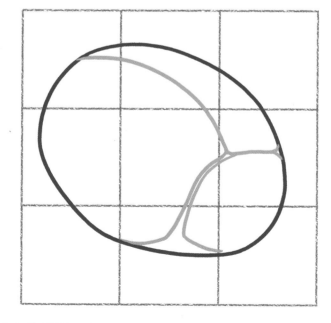

3.

Add big eyes and feet. Draw in the large spots on the back and head to finish.

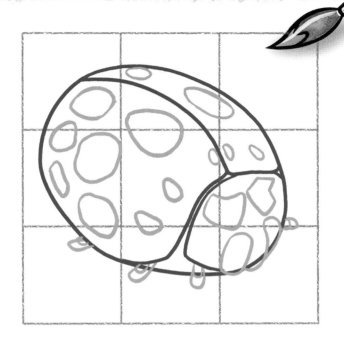

Artist Tip:

Here is a secret to great shading.

1. *The dotted lines represent the section to highlight. You can also highlight the bug's head and eyes. This is colored much lighter than the rest of the bug. The highlight is stronger on one side and fades out a little at the other end.*

2. *Notice that at the edge of the highlight the red is darkest. This color then fades into a brighter red, as it moves away from the highlighted section. This is the same for the body, head and eyes with their colors.*

4.

Color in your ladybug. Notice how there is a little bit of color on the feet.

Dragonfly

Dragonflies are a flying insect and come in many different colors. They live near a source of water, where they lay their eggs. Although they are a large insect, they don't sting or bite humans. The dragonfly eats mainly smaller insects such as mosquitoes and small flies. Some dragonflies can fly up to 38 mph (61 km/h)!

1.

Begin by drawing a grid with three equal squares going across and down.

Next draw the shapes for the head and the body parts. Check these are positioned in the correct place on the grid.

2.

Add the wings on the correct angle. Draw in the tail to finish this stage.

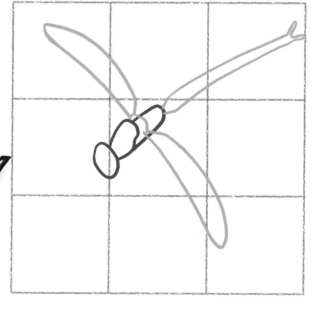

3.

Define the face by drawing in the eyes. Add the front wings and the short strokes for the legs behind the eyes.

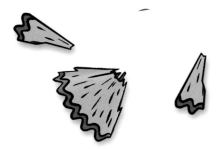

4.

Finish off by drawing the rest of the leg parts and the mouth parts.

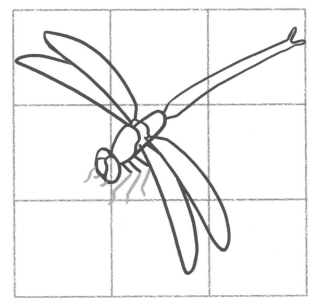

5.

Here we have added some subtle lines for the veins in the wings. Because the wings are thin, drawing these in black would have made our wings appear too dark and heavy.

Cicada

Cicadas can spend six to 17 years underground just growing up. When they come out of the ground, the adult cicadas live for only a few weeks. The male cicada makes the loudest sound in the insect world. If you stand right next to him, he can sound as loud as a lawn mower!

1.

Begin by drawing a grid with four equal squares going across and three down.

Then draw the cicada's strange shaped body and head. Check you have drawn it in the correct place on the grid.

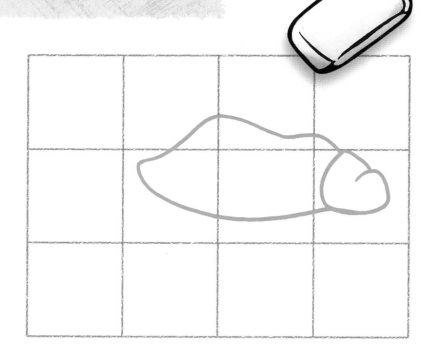

2.

Add the shapes for the wings. Complete this stage by drawing in the eye.

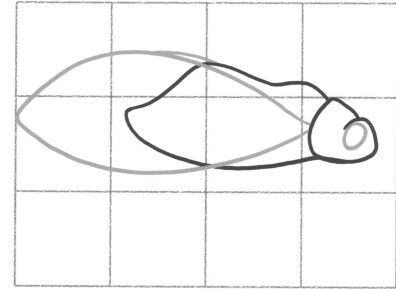

3.

Add the legs, paying close attention to how many parts there are to each leg. Draw in the small antennae.

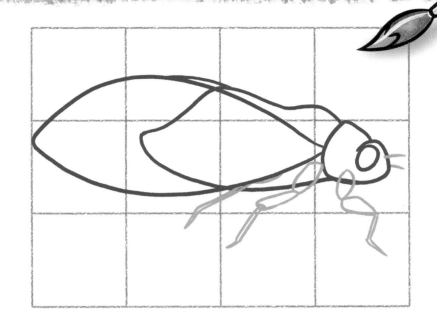

4.

Finish with the veins on the wings. When outlining your drawing, note how the back of the body line is seen through the wings. This makes the wings look transparent.

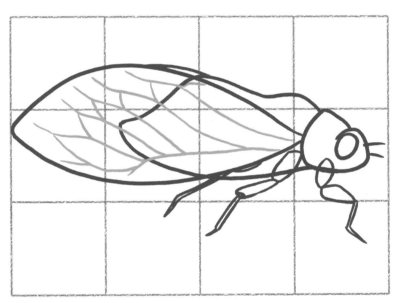

5.

This cicada has been drawn horizontally. You may like to draw the cicada vertically, as if it was hanging onto the trunk of a tree.

Caterpillar

Most caterpillars have 16 legs. They have to watch out for dragonflies and birds who like to eat them. Caterpillars like to eat and eat and eat…they eat constantly and grow quickly as a result. After they finish growing, they spin a shell called a "cocoon" around them like a sleeping bag. When they're inside the cocoon, they turn into a butterfly.

1.

Begin by drawing a grid with four equal squares going across and two down.

Next draw a wobbly cone shape. Be careful to note where the shape crosses each point in the grid.

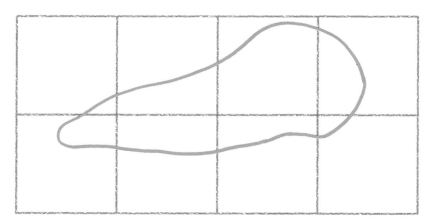

2.

Draw some curved lines that go slightly above the first shape to make it look lumpy. These curve around to form the body.

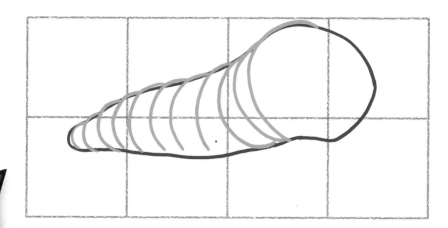

3.

Draw in the rest of the lines around the body. Add the shapes for the feet. Notice how they get smaller the further back they are on the insect?

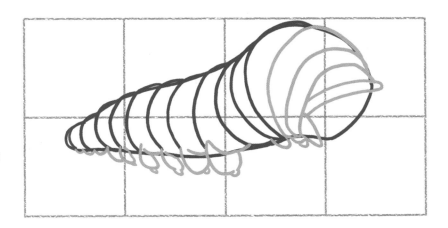

4.

Finish with the details of the face and the lines for the tree.

Now you are ready to outline your drawing and erase the pencil lines.

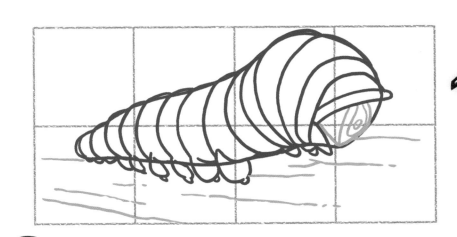

5.

Here we have the caterpillar on a tree branch. You may like to put it on a leaf that has bite marks from the insect munching on it.

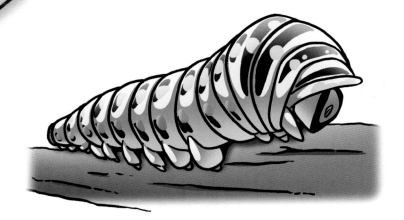

Butterfly

There are about 17,000 different types of butterflies. Most adult butterflies only live for one or two weeks. Their mouth is like a straw so they can reach down into flowers and feed on the nectar. Their mouth is rolled up when they aren't eating. Some butterflies can taste with their feet!

1.

Begin by drawing a grid with four equal squares going across and three down.

Then draw a stretched semicircle and oval near the bottom of the grid.

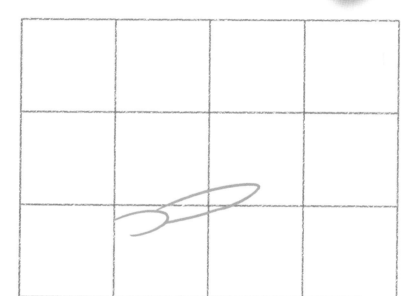

2.

Add the shapes for the face and the eyes. Draw in the shapes for the wings to finish this stage.

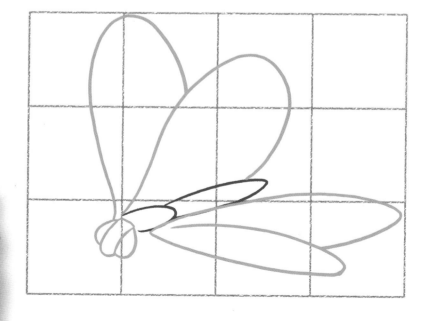

3.

Add the mouth straw at the front of the face. Draw in the legs and underside of the body. Draw lines with arches in them on the wings.

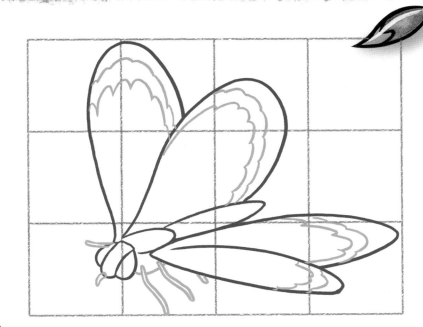

4.

Add the antennae from the top of the head. Draw in lines on the wings to meet the points of the arches drawn in stage 3.

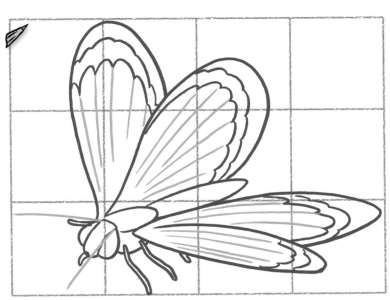

5.

Once you have outlined your butterfly, you may like to color it with many colors. Butterflies are one of the most colorful insects in the world.

Blowfly

Blowflies (or bluebottles) are big noisy flies. They are commonly found at barbecues and picnics trying to land on your burger or swim in your drink. Another place to hang out is the garbage bin. Blowflies are typically unclean, slow, and dopey.

1.

Begin by drawing a grid with three equal squares going across and down.

Now draw a large circle for the body. Add the eyes and face shape above it.

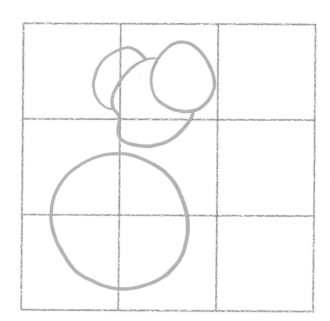

2.

Cut the eye shapes in half with a slightly curved line for eyelids. Draw in a curved line for the pupils. This makes the blowfly look sleepy. Add the rest of the body and the wings on either side.

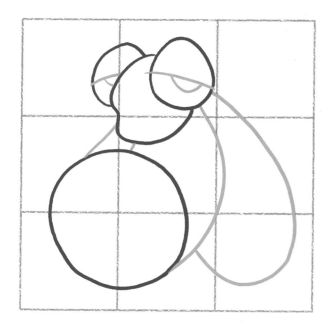

3.

Here we make the eyelids thicker by drawing slightly larger lines around the outside of the eyes. Next add the small mouth parts. Finish this stage with the thin arm and upturned hand.

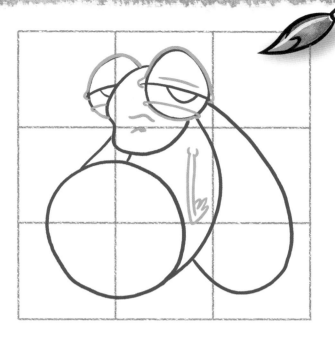

4.

Add two more sets of arms below the first set. Put in some veins on the wings. Use short strokes and dots around the body and face to make the blowfly slightly hairy.

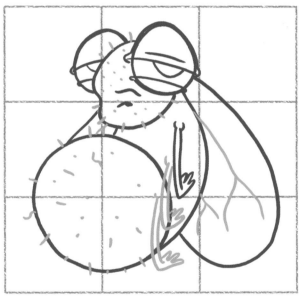

5.

A dull, dreary blue-gray color best suits a fly. This highlights the dullness and greasiness of his character.

Bee

In the bee world, the queen bee is the boss. A worker bee's job is to collect nectar from flowers. They use the nectar to make honey. They all work together to get the job done. Only the female bees can sting and collect honey. The buzzing noise that bees make is their wings flapping really fast.

1.

Begin by drawing a grid with four equal squares going across and three down.

Next, draw the shape for the head. Add the next two shapes, being careful to take note of the size of them.

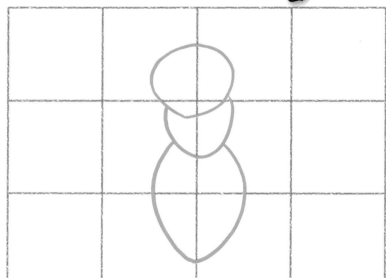

2.

Draw the eyes on the edges of the head shape. Add the folded antennae. Draw in the bucket to finish this stage.

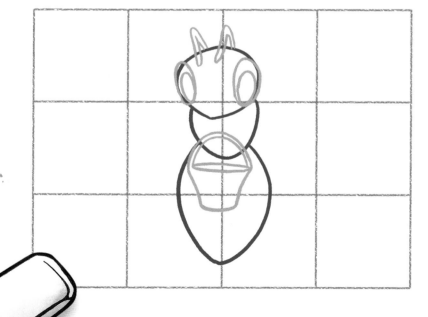

3.

Here we add the arms holding the bucket. Next, draw in the legs, starting at each side of the bucket. Draw in the shapes for the wing movement. Add the highlight on the eyes to finish.

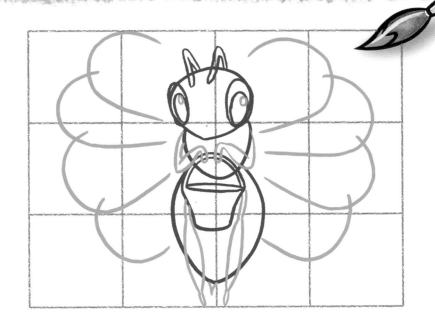

4.

Add the second set of hands and elbows near the bucket. Finish with the movement lines on the wings.

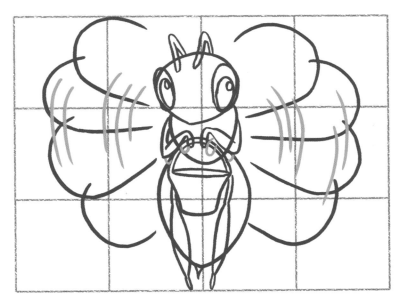

5.

To make this bee look feminine, large eyelashes have been added. This is an easy way to make something look female. Try it with your own drawings.

Bedbug

Bedbugs are actually real insects. They are little bugs that bite like mosquitoes while somebody is sleeping. They don't just live in beds, but also in places like clothes or sofas. Bedbugs are rare these days because people are cleaner and wash a lot more than the average person that lived 100 years ago. Bedbug stories are often told to scare children.

1.

Begin by drawing a grid with four equal squares going across and three down.

Continue this stage by drawing the rectangle for the bed. Draw the folded bed sheets around the middle of this rectangle. Add the shape for the head and mouth.

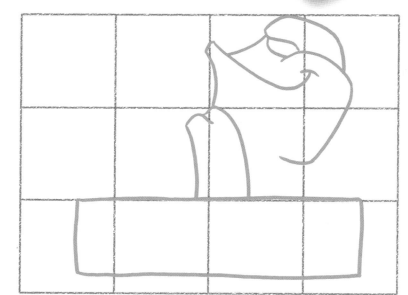

2.

Draw in the shape for the rest of the bed covers. Add the pillow and bulgy mattress. Finish by adding the feet on the bed.

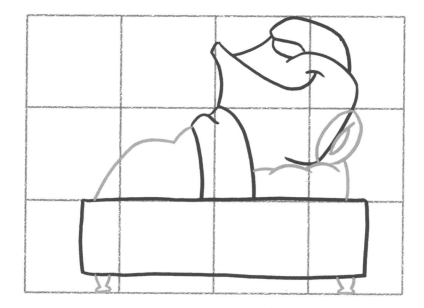

3.

Draw the teeth on the mouth and the eye. Add the shoulder and hand. Draw some ovals on the head to add character. Finish with the headboard and the feet of the bed.

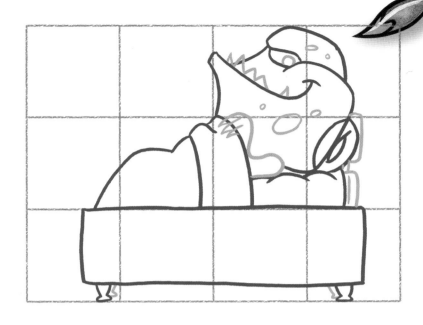

Artist Tip:

Shading can bring a drawing to life. Here is an example of stages of shading.

1. This stage has flat or solid color. There is no shading at all here.

2. Highlights and shadows are added in this stage. Highlights can be pure white or a lighter version of the flat color. We used green for the face so we would use a much lighter green for the highlights on the face. It is the same with shadows. We used a green for the face so we use a much darker green for the shadows on the face.

3. Here a darker color has been applied to show that the bug is in a dark room. Where there were greens, blues and browns, a darker version was colored over them.

4.

To make this bedbug even more dramatic, a dark background has been added with a slightly opened door. "Goodnight! Sleep tight! Don't let the bedbugs BITE!"

Rhino Beetle

The rhino beetle gets its name from the horns that are on its head, which are like real rhinoceros' horns. It lives in rainforests all over the world. The rhino beetle is also really strong. It can carry up to 850 times its own weight! Can you imagine how strong you would have to be to lift 850 kids just like you?

1.

Begin by drawing a grid with three equal squares going across and down.

Draw the large shapes for the head and belly. Be careful to place them in the correct position on the grid.

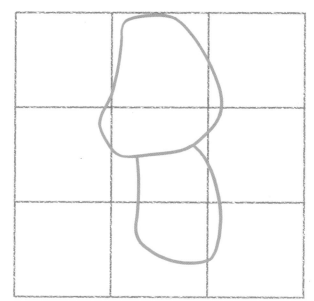

2.

Add the big curved horn. Draw in the shape on the top of his head. Draw the large curve for his shell and add the extra lines. Finish with the part of the shell on the other side of his body.

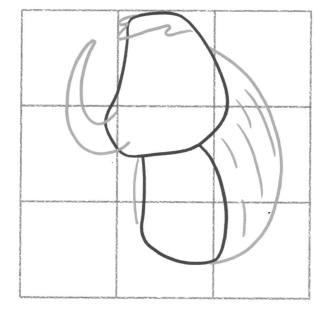

3.

Draw in his eyes. Notice how the further eye is very thin and is on the side of the head shape. Add the mouth and air puff. Draw in the curved legs to finish this stage.

4.

Draw the hands with the dumbbells. Add some movement lines underneath these and some sweat drips on either side of his head.

5.

Rhino beetles are very dark, so try to choose a color that is dark but doesn't block out your black outlines.

Mosquito

Mosquitoes are attracted to sweat, warmth, light, body odor, and the air we breathe out of our lungs. They breed in still water – anything from still creeks to puddles. Only the females can bite and when they do, they leave little, itchy red marks. They also have an annoying buzzing sound, which is heard after you turn your bedroom light off.

1.

Begin by drawing a grid with four equal squares going across and three down.

Next, draw the shapes for the head, body, and tail. Check to make sure you have them in the correct places on the grid.

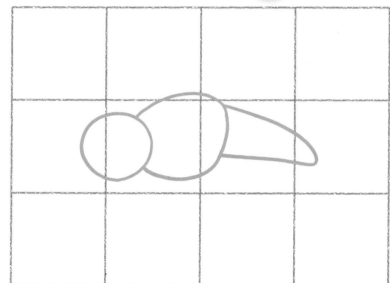

2.

Draw in the eyes and mouth. Add the napkin. Draw in the wings to finish this stage.

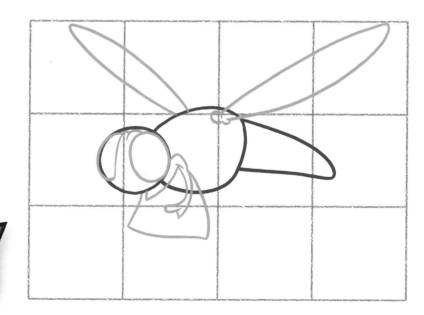

3.

Draw in the swirl on the large eye. Add the eyelid for the other eye. Draw in the snout and circles at the base of the eye. Draw the hairs on the back. Finish with the lines on the wings.

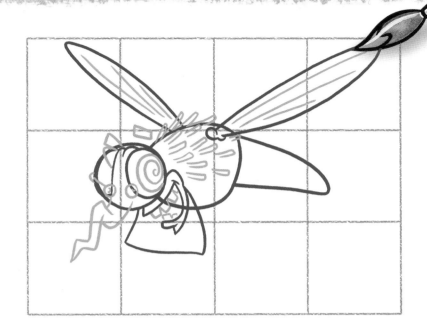

4.

Draw the front legs with the hands and cutlery. Add the pupil in the further eye. Draw the rest of the legs on both sides. Add some rings around the tail to finish.

5.

Mosquitoes are a menacing insect. What better way to capture this characteristic than with a menacing looking mosquito. Good thing they're easy to swat, huh?!

Grasshopper

Some grasshoppers will only eat certain types of leaves, while others will eat almost any type of plant. Grasshoppers sometimes eat so much that farmers can lose all the crops that they have been growing. Grasshoppers can fly, but they are best known for their ability to jump really high and far for their size.

1.

Begin by drawing a grid with four equal squares going across and three down.

Study these shapes carefully in order to recreate them on your own grid. Begin by drawing in the head, eye, and mouth shapes.

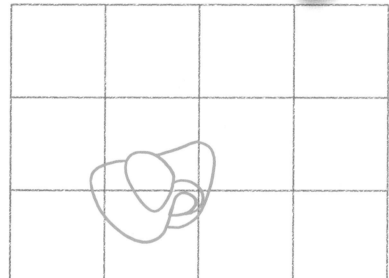

2.

Draw in some lines for the eyelids and the eyeballs. Add the eye shape on the other side of the head shape. Draw the wings and add the lines for the underbelly of the grasshopper.

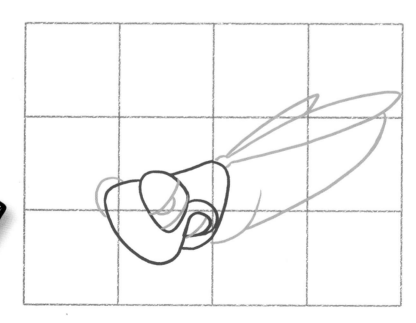

3.

Draw the similar two front legs and their shoes. Draw in the large back leg and shoe to match.

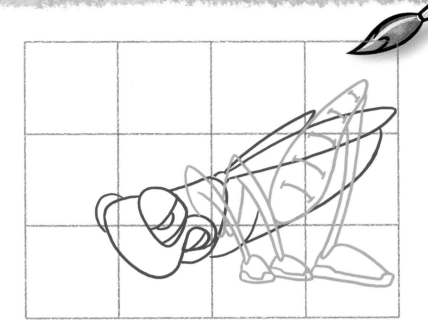

4.

Add the antennae on the head. Draw the legs and shoes on the opposite side. To finish, define the laces on the shoes.

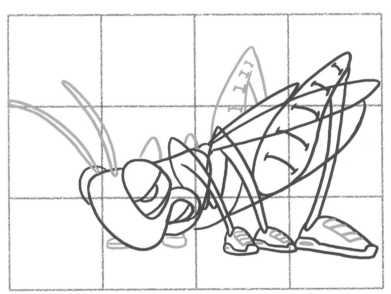

5.

Because grasshoppers can jump so far, we thought it would be fun to enter him into the cartoon insect Olympics. What other insects can you think of to join in these games?

LONGJUMP COMPETITION

Published in 2015 by **Windmill Books,**
an Imprint of Rosen Publishing,
29 East 21st Street, New York, NY 10010.

Written and illustrated by Damien Toll.
With thanks to Jared Gow.

Library of Congress Cataloging-in-Publication Data
Toll, Damien.
 Drawing awesome insects / Damien Toll.
    pages cm. — (Drawing is awesome!)
 Includes index.
 ISBN 978-1-4777-5458-0 (pbk.)
 ISBN 978-1-4777-5474-0 (6 pack)
 ISBN 978-1-4777-5473-3 (library binding)
 1. Insects in art—Juvenile literature.
 2. Drawing—Technique—Juvenile literature.
 I. Title.
 NC783.T65 2015
 743.6'57—dc23

                        2014027094

Manufactured in the United States of America
CPSIA Compliance Information: Batch # CW15WM: For Further Information contact
Rosen Publishing, New York, New York at 1-800-237-9932